A CULINARY JOURNEY

Exploring destinations and discovering different cultures and traditions is at the heart of every Viking journey. And of course food – not only the recipes prepared by our onboard chefs, but also local cuisine in all the fascinating places our ships visit – is an essential part of the overall Viking experience.

We hope this book helps you to recreate the flavors of your travels back home in your own kitchen, and inspires you to continue exploring the world.

THE AMERICAS &
THE CARIBBEAN

Early Native Americans used a variety of cooking methods which were blended with European techniques to form the basis of modern American cuisine. The early colonists farmed meat and had similar cuisine to Europe, although the pioneers had to make use of whatever food was available to them. Multiple ethnic and regional approaches have also had a huge influence on both North and South American cuisine. Similarly, Caribbean cuisine is a melangé of different influences, including the Carib, Arawak and Taino ancient tribes, and Spanish, French, African, Indian and Chinese. Barbecue was actually invented by the Arawaks, who cooked meat on a wood fire so that it imbibed the smoky flavors.

NORTH AMERICA

North American cuisine varies
tremendously from region to region,
drawing on ethnic influences as well
as local produce and climate. The Deep
South has its roots in French and Creole
cuisine; New England is renowned
for its seafood whilst New York has
developed an exciting dining scene.

BOSTON/NEW ENGLAND CLAM CHOWDER

Serves 4

1 oz (30g) butter
6 slices streaky bacon, chopped
2 onions, chopped
3 tbsp flour
1 pint (475ml) chicken stock
1 ¼ lb (565g) tinned clams in brine
2 bay leaves
4 potatoes, peeled and chopped
8 fl oz (235ml) heavy (double) cream
Salt and pepper

TO GARNISH:
2 slices streaky bacon, chopped

1 Heat the butter in a large saucepan. Add the bacon, fry for a couple of minutes, then add the onions and fry for a further five minutes or until just softened.

2 Sprinkle over the flour and stir to combine, then pour over the stock, stirring well. Strain the clams and add the clam liquid into the pot.

3 Add the bay leaves, potatoes and cream and bring to a simmer, stirring regularly, then reduce and cover for about 20 minutes until the potatoes are tender.

4 Meanwhile, fry the remaining two slices of bacon until golden and crispy, then reserve and keep warm.

5 Finally, remove the bay leaves, add the clams and season to taste. Cook just until the clams are heated through, then serve. Garnish with the crispy bacon.

VIKING BURGER

Serves 6

6 sesame-seeded buns
6 slices cheddar cheese
6 slices pancetta
Smoky barbecue sauce

FOR THE BEEF PATTIES:

2 lb (900g) minced beef
1 egg, beaten
1 tbsp Worcestershire
    sauce
2 ½ oz (70g) dry
    breadcrumbs

FOR THE ONION RELISH:

4 tbsp butter
Pinch salt
6 red onions, sliced
6 fl oz (175ml) orange
    juice
3.5 fl oz (100ml) red
    wine vinegar
2 tbsp rice wine vinegar
4 tbsp honey
1 small beet (beetroot)

TO SERVE:

French fries
Coleslaw
Lettuce and tomato
Sweet pickled gherkins

1 To make the burger patties, mix the minced beef, egg, Worcestershire sauce and breadcrumbs together in a large bowl. Shape into six generous burgers, then chill until required.

2 For the red onion relish, melt the butter in a heavy based pan and add in the onions. Sprinkle over the salt, then cook gently until soft and translucent, but not colored. Add in the orange juice and both vinegars, then stir in the honey and the thinly sliced beet.

3 Continue to cook gently until all the excess liquid has evaporated and the mixture has thickened. Allow to cool.

4 Season the burger patties with salt and pepper, then grill for about 3-5 minutes on each side (the exact cooking time will depend on whether you prefer them medium or well done).

5 Meanwhile, toast the burger buns and add a slice of cheddar to the bottom half. Place the cooked burgers onto the cheese to melt. As you remove the burgers, add the slices of pancetta to the grill to crisp up.

6 Top each burger with a generous spoonful of the onion relish and a squeeze of barbecue sauce. Finish with the crispy pancetta before adding the top half of the bun. Serve with French fries, coleslaw, crunchy lettuce and slices of tomato, and a few sweet-pickled gherkins.

CLASSIC MEATLOAF

Serves 6

4 oz (115g) white bread
1 tbsp dehydrated onion
1 tsp garlic granules
1 tsp poultry seasoning
Salt and pepper
4 fl oz (120ml) milk
1.5 lb (680g) lean
  minced beef (around
  15% fat)

1 Preheat the oven to 375°F (190°C).

2 Using a food processor, whizz the bread into breadcrumbs. Place the breadcrumbs in a bowl and add the dehydrated onion, garlic granules, poultry seasoning and milk. Season generously and stir well.

3 Add in the beef and mix thoroughly until everything is well combined. Press the mixture into a 2 lb (900g) non-stick loaf tin. Cover with non-stick baking paper.

4 After half an hour, remove the baking paper, then bake uncovered for a further half hour.

NEW YORK BAKED CHEESECAKE

Serves 6–8

7 oz (200g) graham
crackers (digestive
biscuits), crushed

3 ½ oz (100g) butter

2 ½ oz (70g) superfine
(caster) sugar

2 tbsp cornstarch
(cornflour)

1.2 lb (545g) full fat
cream cheese

2 eggs

2 ½ fl oz (75ml) sour
cream

1 tsp vanilla extract

1 Grease and line an 8 inch (20cm) springform
cake tin and preheat the oven to 350°F (175°C).
Make sure that the cream cheese is at room
temperature to ensure a smooth finish.
2 Place the biscuits in a plastic bag and bash
with a rolling pin until completely crushed. Melt
the butter gently in a saucepan, then mix the
two together and press into the base of the tin.
Bake the base for 10 minutes, then allow to cool.
3 Turn the oven up slightly to 400°F (200°C).
Mix the sugar and cornstarch together, then
using an electric mixer, slowly beat in the cream
cheese until smooth. Add the eggs and beat well
before adding the sour cream and vanilla extract.
4 Stand the tin on a couple of sheets of
aluminium foil and fold up around the tin,
wrapping it so that no water can get in. Spoon
the mixture onto the base and smooth the
surface. Stand the cheesecake in a baking tray
and carefully pour water around it. Bake for 40
to 45 minutes or until golden brown. If the top
starts to get too brown, cover loosely with foil.
Allow to cool completely before serving.

CANADA

With its majestic scenery and stunning wildlife, Canada is rich in natural resources. While Canadian cuisine can be viewed as a collage of dishes from other cultures, smoked meat, Pacific salmon and maple syrup are all popular, and French influences have resulted in some exquisite gastronomy.

POUTINE

Serves 4

Vegetable oil, for frying
5 large potatoes
2 tbsp butter
2 tbsp all purpose
  (plain) flour
2 pints (950ml) good
  quality veal, beef or
  vegetable stock
8 oz (225g) mozzarella,
  shredded, or Cheddar,
  grated

1 Peel the potatoes and cut into thick fries. Place in a bowl, cover with cold water and allow to soak until needed.
2 Heat the oil in a deep fat fryer until it reaches 375°F (190°C).
3 Heat the butter in a heavy-based frying pan and add the flour. Mix well and allow to cook for a few minutes until pale and bubbling, then gradually whisk in the stock until smooth. Allow to simmer until thick and glossy, whisking the mixture frequently.
4 Drain the fries and pat dry with kitchen paper, then fry in the hot oil until golden and crisp. Drain well, then serve immediately, smothered with the gravy and topped with the cheese.

TOURTIÈRE

Serves 4–6

2 tbsp olive oil

1 large onion, finely
   chopped

1 lb (450g) minced pork

8 oz (225g) minced beef

1 large potato, peeled
   and cut into small dice

½ tsp ground cinnamon

½ tsp ground cloves

Salt and pepper

Nutmeg, grated

6 fl oz (175ml) beef
   stock

FOR THE PASTRY:

7 oz (200g) cold butter

14 oz (400g) all purpose
   (plain) flour

1 egg

TO GLAZE:

1 egg, whisked

Salt and pepper

1 Heat the oil in a large, heavy based frying pan and fry the onion for about 10 minutes until soft and lightly golden. Add the pork and beef mince to the pan and combine well, breaking it up and allowing it to brown all over.

2 Stir in the potato and spices, season well with the salt and pepper and add a generous grating of nutmeg, then pour over the stock. Reduce the heat, cover and simmer for about 30 minutes, stirring occasionally, until most of the liquid is absorbed. Check the seasoning, then allow to cool and refrigerate.

3 To make the pastry, cut the butter into cubes and place in a bowl with the flour and a pinch of salt. Rub gently with your fingertips until the mixture resembles breadcrumbs. Add the egg and stir gently until the mixture comes together (you may need one or two tablespoons of cold water). Form the dough gently into two balls, wrap and chill for about 20 minutes.

4 To assemble the pie, first preheat the oven to 375°F (190°C). Roll the pastry out into two discs about ¼ inch (6mm) thick. Use the first circle to line a 9 inch (23cm) pie dish. Add the filling, pressing it down lightly, then cover with the second piece of dough. Wet the edges and crimp all around to seal, then make a small hole at the center of the pie with the tip of a knife.

5 Whisk the egg, season with salt and pepper and brush generously all over the pie. Bake for an hour until golden brown.

ALASKA

The largest state of the USA is
characterized by its vast open spaces,
sweeping forests and stunning
mountain ranges. At the center of its
cuisine is cold-water seafood,
in particular salmon, which is
served smoked, cured, baked, or
even as salmon jerky.

BROWN SUGAR GLAZED ALASKAN SALMON

Serves 4

2 tbsp butter
1 tbsp brown sugar
1 tsp honey
½ lemon, juice only
1 tbsp Dijon mustard
1 tbsp soy sauce
Salt and freshly ground
  pepper
1 large side of salmon
  (allow 6-8 oz/170-225g
  per person)

1 Preheat the oven to 350°F (175°C).

2 Melt the butter, brown sugar and honey in a small saucepan over a low heat. Remove from the heat and whisk in the lemon juice, mustard, and soy sauce. Season to taste and allow to cool.

3 Place the salmon on a large baking sheet lined with baking paper. Brush the glaze generously all over the salmon. Bake for 20 to 25 minutes or until cooked through.

THE CARIBBEAN

A colorful blend of turquoise waters
and lush emerald green islands, the
Caribbean is known for its hot and
spicy cuisine. A fusion of African,
Native American, European, east
Indian, Arab and Chinese influences,
Caribbean recipes usually involve rice,
plantains, cilantro, bell peppers, chick
peas, sweet potatoes and coconut.

CALLALOO

Serves 4

1 lb (450g) fresh
  Callaloo
2 tbsp vegetable oil
3 garlic cloves, crushed
1 onion, sliced
3 scallions (spring
  onions), chopped
1 sprig of fresh thyme
Salt and black pepper
  to taste
2 ½ fl oz (75ml) water

1 Cut any tough stems from the leaves and allow to soak for a few minutes in cold water. Drain, then roughly slice.

2 Heat the oil in a large saucepan, then add the garlic, onion and scallions. Fry until just beginning to soften, then add the leaves, the sprig of thyme and a generous amount of salt and black pepper. Pour over the water and cover. Cook for about 8 to 10 minutes, stirring occasionally, until the stems are tender. Serve with fried plantains.

JERK CHICKEN

Serves 4–6

2 scotch bonnet or
  jalapeño chili peppers,
  chopped
2 tbsp thyme
1 tbsp ground allspice
4 cloves garlic, chopped
1 tsp fresh ginger,
  grated
2 tbsp honey
2 tsp salt
2 tsp ground black
  pepper
1 lime, juiced
1 ½ fl oz (45ml) olive oil
4 chicken breasts,
  cubed, or 1 whole
  chicken, cut into pieces

1 Place all the ingredients apart from the chicken in a blender and process until smooth. Pour the marinade over the chicken and allow to marinate for at least an hour.

2 Either grill the marinated chicken on a barbecue until cooked through, or bake in the oven at 400°F (200°C) for 25 to 30 minutes, turning half way through the cooking time. Serve immediately with rice 'n' peas, or with a side dish of Callaloo.

RUM PUNCH

Serves 1

¾ fl oz (25ml) lime juice
1 ½ fl oz (45ml) sugar
  cane syrup
2 ¼ fl oz (65ml) dark
  Jamaican rum
3 fl oz (90ml) water
A sprinkling of freshly
  grated nutmeg

1 In a wide glass tumbler, combine all the ingredients over ice cubes and stir well.
2 To make a larger batch, use the tumbler to measure each ingredient into a jug (one cup of lime juice, two cups of sugar cane syrup, three cups of rum, and so on).

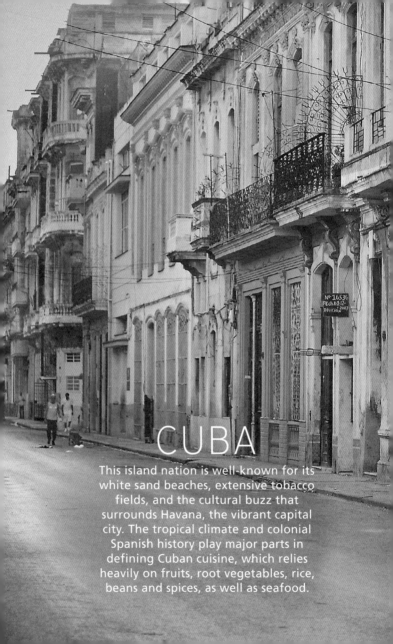

CUBA

This island nation is well-known for its white sand beaches, extensive tobacco fields, and the cultural buzz that surrounds Havana, the vibrant capital city. The tropical climate and colonial Spanish history play major parts in defining Cuban cuisine, which relies heavily on fruits, root vegetables, rice, beans and spices, as well as seafood.

CUBA LIBRE

Serves 1

¾ fl oz (25ml) Bacardi
  white rum
2 wedges fresh lime
3 fl oz (90ml) Coca Cola,
  chilled
Fresh lime, sliced, to
  garnish

1 Fill a highball glass with ice, then pour over the rum. Squeeze over the lime wedges and add to the glass. Top with chilled Coca Cola. Stir and serve, garnished with a slice of fresh lime.

FRICASÉ DE POLLO

Serves 4

1 large chicken,
jointed and skinned
(or 4 lb/1.8kg chicken
pieces)
4 fl oz (120ml) sour
(Seville) orange juice
(or use ½ orange,
½ lime)
4 cloves garlic, whole
1 tsp salt
½ tsp freshly ground
black pepper
2-3 tbsp all purpose
(plain) flour
2 tbsp olive oil
2 large onions, chopped
1 green bell pepper,
deseeded and chopped
½ tsp dried oregano
1 glass dry white wine
1 lb (450g) red potatoes,
peeled and chopped
½ can (7 oz/200g)
crushed tomatoes
3 ½ oz (100g) pimento
stuffed green olives
2 ½ oz (70g) raisins

1 Place the chicken pieces in a non-metallic bowl and pour over the citrus juice. Smash the unpeeled garlic cloves but keep them whole and add them to the bowl along with the salt and pepper. Cover and refrigerate for one to two hours to let the flavors develop.

2 Remove the chicken (reserving the marinade). Peel and crush the garlic cloves.

3 Pat the chicken dry with kitchen paper, then dust lightly with flour. In a heavy-based pan or Dutch oven, heat the oil, then add in the chicken pieces. Fry a couple at a time in the oil until golden brown, then remove with a slotted spoon and keep warm.

4 Add the chopped onions, pepper, oregano and the crushed garlic in to the pan. Fry gently, adding a little more oil if necessary, until softened. Deglaze the pan with the wine, scraping the bottom of the pan and allowing it to cook out for a couple of minutes.

5 Pour in the reserved marinade along with the chicken, potatoes, crushed tomatoes, olives and raisins. Bring to the boil, then reduce the heat, cover and cook for around 30 minutes. Serve over rice.

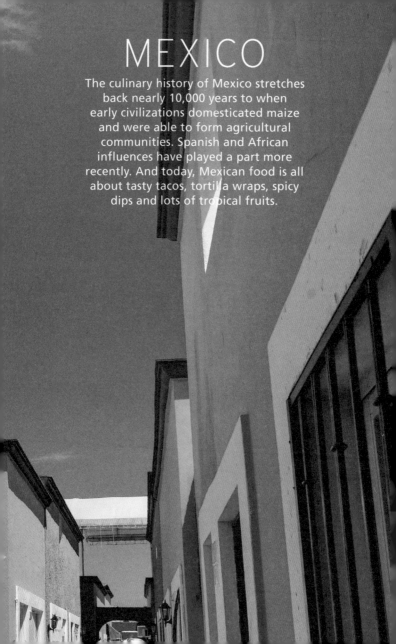

MEXICO

The culinary history of Mexico stretches back nearly 10,000 years to when early civilizations domesticated maize and were able to form agricultural communities. Spanish and African influences have played a part more recently. And today, Mexican food is all about tasty tacos, tortilla wraps, spicy dips and lots of tropical fruits.

CHILI CON CARNE

Serves 4

2 tbsp olive oil

1 large onion, peeled
and finely chopped

2 dried ancho chilies,
soaked, deseeded and
chopped

2 cloves garlic, minced

1 carrot, finely chopped

1 stick of celery, finely
chopped

Salt and pepper

1 lb (450g) lean minced
beef

1 tsp cumin

1 tsp hot chili powder

1 pint (475ml) passata
(or 1 can tomatoes,
chopped)

15 oz (425g) tin kidney
beans, drained

1 Heat the oil in a large, heavy-based frying pan
on a medium heat and add in the onion, chilies,
garlic, carrot and celery. Season with salt and
pepper and fry gently for six to eight minutes
until the mix has softened.

2 Add in the minced beef, breaking it up with
the spoon and allowing it to brown all over.
Then sprinkle over the cumin and chili powder.

3 Stir in the passata, and the drained kidney
beans, then rinse the container out with
6 ½ fl oz (200ml) water and add to the pan.
Cook until the liquid reaches a slow simmer.
Turn the heat down, cover and allow to cook for
an hour, stirring occasionally.

4 Serve with a generous spoonful of sour cream
and some fluffy white rice.

VEGETARIAN CHILI

To adapt this recipe for vegetarians, substitute
8 oz (225g) red split lentils for the minced beef
and add 1 red pepper, deseeded and chopped.

GUACAMOLE

Serves 4

2 large, ripe avocados
1 medium red onion,
  finely chopped
2 large ripe tomatoes,
  deseeded and chopped
1 jalapeño chili pepper,
  deseeded and chopped
1 lime, juiced
Large bunch fresh
  cilantro (coriander),
  chopped
Salt and pepper to taste

1 De-stone the avocados, then scoop out the flesh into the bowl of a mortar. Add in the onion, tomatoes and chili and bash with the pestle until well combined.
2 Add lime juice, salt and pepper to taste. Serve immediately with tortilla chips.

CHILE

Sandwiched between the Andes
mountain range and the Pacific Ocean,
this long, thin country has a varied
climate that results in a wide range
of agricultural produce and seafood.
Colonial Spanish influences are mixed
with traditional indigenous dishes to
form a vibrant cuisine. Chilean wine is
also a world-famous export.

EMPANADAS DE PINO

Makes 12

FOR THE DOUGH:

8 fl oz (235ml) milk

4 oz (115g) vegetable
shortening (or butter)

1 tsp salt

2 egg yolks

1 lb (450g) all purpose
(plain) flour

FOR THE FILLING:

2 tbsp oil

2 large onions, chopped

2 cloves garlic, crushed

1 lb (450g) ground
(minced) beef

1 tsp ground cumin

1 tsp chili powder

2 tsp paprika

1 tsp salt

½ tsp freshly ground
black pepper

2 fl oz (60ml) beef stock

2 tbsp all purpose
(plain) flour

2-3 tbsp raisins

2-3 tbsp black olives,
chopped

2 hard-boiled eggs,
chopped

1 egg, beaten

1 First, make the dough. Heat the milk gently in a saucepan until just warm. Add in the shortening and salt. Turn off the heat, stirring until just lukewarm then mix in the egg yolks.

2 Place the flour in a large bowl, make a well in the center then pour in the milk mixture. Bring together into a soft dough, adding extra flour if necessary. Knead the dough until smooth. Cover with plastic wrap and set aside.

3 Heat the oil in a large frying pan. Add in the onions and fry gently until soft but not colored, then add in the garlic and fry briefly.

4 Add the beef to the pan, breaking it up with a wooden spoon, then sprinkle over the spices, salt and pepper. Pour over the stock and stir it all together for 10 minutes until the meat is cooked through. Add the raisins and sprinkle over the flour, then continue to cook until the sauce is thickened. Taste for seasoning and allow to cool.

5 Preheat the oven to 350°F (175°C). To make the empanadas, roll the dough and divide into 12 equal pieces. Roll each one into a ball, then on a floured surface, roll out into a small circle (about 6 inches/15cm across).

6 Place a tablespoon of the mixture in the top half of the circle, then add some chopped boiled egg. Moisten the edges with a little water, then fold the pastry over the filling to make a semi-circle. Seal the edges, starting at one end and gently rolling up the edge (or press with a fork).

7 Brush the empanadas with beaten egg then bake for 25-30 minutes until golden brown.

PEBRE

4 scallions (spring
onions), finely
chopped
3 cloves garlic, crushed
Large bunch cilantro
(coriander), leaves
only, chopped
2 tbsp red wine vinegar
3 tbsp red chili pepper
paste (or freshly
minced red chili
peppers)
2 tbsp olive oil
½ tsp sea salt
½ tsp freshly ground
black pepper
1 lime, juiced

1 Add the scallions, garlic, cilantro, red wine
vinegar, chili paste and olive oil to a bowl. Stir
well and season with salt and pepper.
2 Add lime juice to taste. Serve on bread or to
accompany grilled meats and fish.

First published in Germany in 2018 by Viking

Copyright © Viking

ISBN 978-1-909968-37-0

Book design by The Chelsea Magazine Company Limited

Photography: James Murphy
Additional images: AWL Images, Getty Images, iStock, StockFood
Recipe testing: Rebecca Wiggins

Printed and bound in Germany by Mohn Media

vikingcruises.com